Dharma
Talk

DHARMA TALK

John Brehm

Foreword by Joseph Goldstein

Wisdom

Wisdom Publications
132 Perry Street
New York, NY 10014 USA
wisdomexperience.org

Library of Congress Cataloging-in-Publication Data
Names: Brehm, John, 1955– author. | Goldstein, Joseph, 1944– writer
    of foreword.
Title: Dharma talk / John Brehm; foreword by Joseph Goldstein.
Description: First edition. | New York: Wisdom Publications, 2023.
Identifiers: LCCN 2023013544 (print) |
    LCCN 2023013545 (ebook) | ISBN 9781614298786 (paper-
    back) | ISBN 9781614298861 (ebook)
Subjects: LCSH: Buddhism—Poetry
Classification: LCC PS3602.R444 D43 2023 (print) | LCC PS3602.
    R444 (ebook) | DDC 811/.6—dc23/eng/20230530
LC record available at https://lccn.loc.gov/2023013544
LC ebook record available at https://lccn.loc.gov/2023013545

ISBN 978-1-61429-878-6   ebook ISBN 978-1-61429-886-1

27 26 25 24 23   5 4 3 2 1

Cover design by Jess Morphew. Interior design by Tim Holtz. Set in
Adobe Caslon Pro and Mrs Eaves.

For Heather Sellers

Contents

III

Foreword

As a poet and longtime student of the Dharma, John Brehm weaves together timeless wisdom and a deep poetic sensibility. The language of his poetry is spare and unadorned and transforms the simplest of experiences into intriguing contemplations of the heart, of the mind, and of awareness itself. He brings fresh perspectives, as well, to traditional Buddhist themes of no-self and emptiness.

John's work reminds me of the great Japanese haiku poets: their attention to the smallest details, compression of language, and a rich appreciation of nature and the human condition. In addition to his longer poems, this volume also includes a dozen haikus that highlight John's creative exploration of this form.

> I put my glasses on
> to see the fog
> more clearly

And:

> coming unstitched—
> even the fake flowers
> grow old

Underpinning all of his work is a warm and compassionate heart, feeling the ten thousand joys and ten thousand sorrows of our life's journey, as well as the liberating humor embedded in our many human foibles. In his poem "Metta," he observes the passersby, offering lovingkindness but unable to refrain from making critical comments as well:

> May you be well, may you be safe,
> may you be happy ... and maybe also
> lose the frowning-into-the-phone
> facial expression I get so tired
> of seeing everywhere I go.

The poem traces the arc from the judgmental mind—"I keep on in this way, dishing out / blessings with a side of helpful advice"—to a feeling that fully expresses what love and compassion are all about when he notices a young woman crying in the café:

> and then I'm in the thick of it,
> wishing her to be well, to be safe,
> to be happy, as if my life
> depended on it.

The title of this book—*Dharma Talk*—perfectly expresses the range and depth of John's poetry. The Dharma does indeed talk to us through this wonderful offering, a seamless blend of art and wisdom.

Joseph Goldstein

I

Morning Dilemma

Awake at four this morning.
Outside it's dark and rainy.
Nothing's visible
beyond a few sketchy trees,
a white fluorescent streetlight
one block over like
a chunk of moon lodged in
winter branches. A day to stay
inside and read a novel
about almost-human
robots. Thank God for novelists.
Old age would be
insupportable without them.
Meditate, read novels, write poems
now and then, stare out the
window, love my wife:
that's my plan for growing old,
my ambition. A ladybug
walked across my desk
a few minutes ago.
Do they fly around in the cold
rain of December? I considered
sliding a piece of paper
under it, opening the window,
and flicking it into

the outer darkness, like a word
flying off a page, but wondered
if it might prefer to stay inside
where it's warm and dry.
And in any case, I would
have had to dislodge my cat,
and she had one foreleg
draped over her eyes,
as if the world were already
too much to bear, which it is,
and while I was struggling
with that decision, the ladybug
moved itself out of my
field of vision, eliminating
the problem without solving it.
Such was the morning's drama
and dilemma—
darkness outside, a visitor
from the insect world, isolated
sharp light illuminating
a chalice of stripped branches,
a man with a cat on his lap
considering it all—
who's to say we weren't
a single being in that moment,

a moment of miraculous
consciousness spread across,
bestowed upon, arising from
these things I have seen and
named and briefly touch
with my mind before
the day begins.

Sleep Thief

My wife had the brilliant idea
to put jasmine blossoms
beside the bed
to help carry me off
to sleep and keep me there
all night long—
sleep, blessed sleep,
like the elegant doe
you catch sight of
in the forest and then
it bounds away
—but in the night
my cat ate my wife's
brilliant idea
and stepped right over
my spinning head
and curled herself into
a black spiral
of unimpeded slumber
and thought nothing of it.

Wishful Thinking

I wish I could lift my brain
from my skull, rest it
in a bowl of cool water,
watch the steam rise,
listen to it sizzle—the poor,
reckless, overheated thing,
always worrying, always wanting.
I would bathe it in sea salt
and lavender, rose oil
and eucalyptus, cradle it
against my chest like a child,
this thing crafted and crazed
by five million years of fear,
the lions that stalked us
on the African savannahs
now internalized.

In its place would be
a space where nothing
could happen,
an attic room with pitched
ceilings and dormer windows
looking out on falling snow,
elm trees etched into

a metallic winter sky,
absolute silence.

A dream house, warm
enclosure and cold clarity
sailing into the wind,

no one at the helm.

Wanting Not Wanting

I wish I didn't
want things

to be other
than they are

but wanting
to be some-

one who
doesn't want

things to be
other than

they are is
just another

way of wanting
things to be

other than
they are—

and I don't
want that.

Dharma Talk

He said changing nothing changes
everything, which if you change

the words around also suggests
that changing everything

changes nothing,
which further implies

that nothing and everything
are interchangeable, are

in fact the same thing, or
the same non-thing, having

no fixed, unchanging nature,
or a nature that is in constant

change, if change can be said
to be constant, and is therefore

a kind of emptiness about
which it is better to speak

only in the negative, of
what it is not, or not

to speak at all.

Vanishing Act

I want what
I say to

be next
to nothing—

I mean
right

next to
nothing

rubbing its
skinny

shoulders
against

infinite
white abyss.

Emptiness Is Not Enough

"Emptiness is not enough," you said,
and we all laughed at that, filling the air
with an ancient human sound.
Funny how we never think
of hunter-gatherers laughing,
but they must have, all that time
lying around singing and fucking,
there must have been laughter, too—
monkey business, Paleolithic slapstick.
Has anyone studied the evolution
of laughter, of humor? Probably.
Is there anything we *haven't* studied,
haven't dragged into the realm of
human comprehension? Even
emptiness: whole books on it,
many talks, six-week online courses,
nine-day retreats. Not that we will
ever know all there is to know
about the empty knowing that pervades
all things. Some neuroscientists
now believe the only way to solve
"the hard problem of consciousness,"
how we get from unconscious matter
to subjective awareness, is by positing
that all matter is, to one degree or another,

conscious, and that human consciousness
is just a scaling up (in some cases
a scaling down) of the consciousness
that's already present in trees and grass, ants
and antelope. Panpsychism is what such
a philosophical position is called, a modern
version of what our distant ancestors
knew to be true, that everything is alive
with spirit, intelligence, sacredness.
Still, one might ask why matter is conscious,
why is there consciousness at all?
An unanswerable question, also known
as a mystery. But why am I saying all this,
suddenly giving a little lecture on a subject
I can just barely pretend to almost understand?
Infinite causes and conditions brought me
to this moment, who can untangle them?
Last night, just before sleep, I prayed
for inspiration, for a poem to be given to me,
and this is what has arisen from the emptiness,
the shape my wish has taken. That would be
one way to explain it. The other ways
are beyond me.

Steady Going

Her cane like
a question

mark
troubling

the side-
walk until

she comes
to a full

stop before
the curb

and trembles
looking out

across the
crossing

a dark blue
brace from

knee to ankle
but her

white-haired
daughter

curves a
hand

on her
low back

to steady her
a gesture

of such
exquisite

comfort
encouragement

direction
I feel it

even here:
it holds me up.

Flight Path

Steadiness
is a virtue

yes but un-
steadiness

also has
its uses—

the butterfly's
wobbly

flight for
example

which is its
only defense

against
predators

like my cat
who leaps

and swipes
and misses

unable
to track its

jagged
trajectory—

how did
nature know

to embody
such perfectly

calibrated
imperfections

in this dreamy
creature

Chuang-Tzu
dreamt of

or was dreamt
up by so

long ago and
which I

(possibly
also my cat)

am dreaming
of now?

Epistemologies

The house
sparrow

does not
know

that I
do not

know
what the

house
sparrow knows.

Decomposition

Framed in the
upended

triangle
of the

dead pine's
now un-

grasping
roots

a cluster
of larkspur

perfectly
composed.

The Things We Tell Each Other

Now that the sky blurs to a sulfurous, apocalyptic
yellow, filled with what our ancient forests
have become, smoke and ash, ghost and accusation,
the constant nerve-grinding flight of helicopters
that ruined every possible silence—aerial tours,
life flights, police surveillance?—has finally ceased.
And so there is one silver lining to our charred
nightmare, the others remain to be seen.
A friend said, *I think it's good the earth
is getting rid of the inflammation inside her.
Unfortunate that life on the outside has to suffer.*
Another said something about *burning through
our karma.* As if finding the right metaphor
would make it all make sense, turn it into an idea,
something to be thought about, cool to the touch.
United in muted anger, even the crows are quiet.
Houses half a block away slip into the unseen,
and the dreamlike nature of reality
the Buddha spoke about now seems quite real,
no longer hidden, though of course nothing
is what it seems, not even our illusions.
We drove down from the mountain the night
the fires started, through darkened towns strewn
with branches, power out, stoplights blank, wind
shaking the car, and I felt I was watching it all

from a distance, nightly news coverage
of a routine disaster involving other people,
except that I was in it this time.
My contemplations on impermanence have not
been deep enough, apparently, because whole towns
dematerializing overnight, a million acres scorched,
fifty thousand people fleeing in terror, still seems
like something that should not be happening.
But the curandero says *the universe knows what it's doing,*
and *the collective awakening is a done deal.*
It's beautiful, the things we tell each other,
the things we think to say. All I know is that
I've been working on this poem for four days
and now the smoke has almost cleared. The sky
is open for business. The choppers are back.

Metta

The book I'm reading suggests we send
lovingkindness to everyone we see,
silently addressing them thus:
"May you be well, may you be safe,
may you be happy." And I do this
for a while, sitting inside a cafe,
watching the foot traffic go by.
It feels good—generous,
loving, kind. But after a time
I start modifying the blessing:
"May you be well, may you be safe,
may you be happy ... and maybe also
lose the frowning-into-the-phone
facial expression I get so tired
of seeing everywhere I go."
It's the shadow side of lovingkindness
sticking its nose in, having its say,
and I can't seem to shut it up.
Someone else walks by and I offer:
"May you be well, may you be safe,
may you be happy ... and while you're at it,
how about some nicer clothes?
It wouldn't kill you to dress
with a bit more panache, would it?"
I keep on in this way, dishing out

blessings with a side of helpful advice,
until I notice across the room two young women
sitting side by side, talking quietly,
in no need of either my good wishes
or my corrective commentary.
But then I see that one of them is crying,
nodding her head when her friend
says something, wiping tears
from her cheeks with the palms
of her hands. She pulls it together
for awhile, but then her face clenches
and she gives in, until her friend
lays a hand on her shoulder
and she can talk again—a gentle
rhythm of crying and talking,
waves rising and falling.
It doesn't look like she's been
visited by tragedy, a sudden death
or shattering diagnosis.
Ordinary heartbreak would be
my guess, the shock of betrayal,
some painful reversal in the endless
cycle of loss and gain, and now
a new emptiness spreads out before her
and she doesn't know what to do.

But what kills me is when she tucks her hair
behind her ear and tries *not* to cry,
and fails, overcome by this sadness,
so that I feel it, too, a great swell lifts
and carries me and almost pulls me under—
and then I'm in the thick of it,
wishing her to be well, to be safe,
to be happy, as if my life
depended on it.

II

cold spring morning—
close the window
    or listen to the warbler?

not so different—
veined spring leaf
and my ancient hand

feet hurt, back hurts,
head hurts—
balanced, at least!

coming unstitched—
even the fake flowers
grow old

I put my glasses on
to see the fog
more clearly

scattered crocuses
as if someone had planted
birdsong

fifty years ago: seeds,
before that, nothing—
    oak trees outside my window

the pain is still there
weeping willow
    my father cut down

lost in a fantasy—
the framed kanji for compassion
falls to the floor

regretting something I said
I turn the lampshade
to hide the seam

sleepless night
Buddha unbothered
on the altar

gently with an upturned broom
guiding the hummingbird
out the window

III

Non-harming

I wonder what the neighbors think when they see me
outside with a BB gun shooting at the pigeons
on our roof. I gave them a copy of my anthology,
The Poetry of Impermanence, Mindfulness, and Joy,
and the introduction makes me sound like
a person who probably wouldn't be shooting
at pigeons, even if only with a BB gun,
which doesn't really hurt them (I tell myself)
but simply encourages them to find
someplace else to deposit their smeary droppings
that threaten to turn one side of our house
into a bad Jackson Pollock painting.
"Honey, come look at this—isn't that
the mindfulness guy out there with a rifle,
shooting at his own house?" I'm well aware
of the irony, but life's like that, isn't it?
A contradiction wrapped in an absurdity, etc.
Still, plunking pigeons with a BB gun
might not fall afoul of the injunction
to not cause harm. (I thought about shooting
myself in the foot just to see how much
it hurt but decided against it.) I tried
placing scary-looking plastic owls strategically
around the roof but the pigeons laughed at that.
I tried an electronic device that sent out

a kind of sub-audible (to humans) shrieking,
imitative of a bird of prey, but they didn't fall for that
either. I always thought pigeons were dumb,
but now I'm not so sure. They've outsmarted me
so far, not that that's any great accomplishment,
moving from one side of the roof to the other,
where the angle for firing is not so good,
and where the homeowner is exposed,
even in this early morning half-light,
to the watchful eyes of the neighbors.

Bomb Pops!

Bomb Pops! were all the rage when I was a kid,
cheerful concoctions of sugar, ice, and
high fructose corn syrup in the shape
of a bomb you could eat.
I loved them, the sound of them,
the low vowel rumble of *Bomb*
followed by the sharp, upward-leaping
explosion of *Pop!* I loved the heft
and shape of them, the rounded top
and ridged sides, more like a rocket,
really. And I loved the colors:
red, blue, and red, white & blue.
But now I wonder who dreamed them up,
how the idea for a bomb-shaped popsicle
hatched itself in some confectionery-
designer's brain and then got approved
by men sitting around a conference table,
some of them no doubt World War II veterans,
and then became so popular, delivered to America's
neighborhoods by milk-white ice-cream trucks
with their Pavlovian circus jingles that lit
the street with children. Was it a subtle,
sinister plan to make war and bombing seem
normal and fun? To rob the word of its meaning,

obscure the purpose of the thing it named,
substitute for shattered bodies
and burning cities a submerged memory
of summery sweetness? Would food
executives in the 1950s have thought like that?
Whatever the reason, they were just so
thoroughly American, *Bomb Pops!*,
combining all the obliviousness and arrogance
and unwavering worship of violence
of a country that had done plenty of bombing
but never, except for Pearl Harbor, been bombed.
(They wouldn't have gone over so well
in London or Dresden or Hiroshima).
Of course I wouldn't have thought of that back then.
I turned my tongue blue many a July afternoon
in Lincoln, Nebraska, licking that ice-cold
bomb-on-a-stick, innocent of everything save
the water balloon wars I organized against
the kids who lived on the lower half
of Scott Avenue, and the pop-bottle rockets
I sometimes shot through a copper tube
from the roof of our house

at my enemies.

Dudley Ball

In third grade only two kids got chased
around the playground.
One was a shaggy-haired boy,
I think his name was Peter,
who miraculously appeared in Lincoln,
Nebraska, from England, in 1963,
trailing clouds of Beatle-mania.
I watched in helpless amazement
as the girls squealed and took off
after him at every recess.
Hard to imagine what they would
have done had they caught him.
Held him down and kissed him?
Torn him limb from limb
like the maenads in Ovid?
The other was Dudley Ball, whose
yellowish face and bloodshot eyes
I now know indicated jaundice
and liver disease but at the time
signified only strangeness,
laughable ugliness, untouchable
difference from the rest of us.
The other boys chased him,
threw kickballs at him, thrilled
they could zing a ball at a weird kid

named Dudley Ball. "Hey Dudley,
have a ball!" "Dudley Ball, what a dud!"
The red hair and freckles, puffy cheeks
and constant perspiration, amplified
his otherness. No one spoke to him.
But why do I see his face so clearly now,
the fear and loneliness in his eyes?
The faces of all the others I've forgotten.
I was outraged at the injustice of it,
the cruelty of the schoolyard taunts.
I told the teacher but can't recall
if she did anything about it.
And then he stopped coming to school.
A few months later, we learned he had died.
I wish now I'd said a kind word
to him, tried harder to protect him.
I had my own strangenesses,
though mine were mostly invisible.
I wish I'd put my arm around his shoulder,
asked him to eat his lunch with me.
We could have watched together
the screeching girls, their mad pursuit,
and marveled at the vagaries of luck
and circumstance that exalt some
and cast down others, dealing out

adoration and ridicule in unequal measure.
We wouldn't have talked that way
back then, of course. More likely
we would have sat in awkward silence,
or talked about what we wanted
to be when we grew up.
Or maybe compared our cowlicks—
I remember now how alike ours were,
a cresting ocean wave on
the right side of our foreheads,
as though we'd each been licked
by the same thick-tongued cow,
a calm old cow who saw all our fears
and flaws and loved us
just the same.

Design

Strung be-
tween

rose
bushes

lit with
late

afternoon
light

this spider
web

pushed
and pulled

by the breeze
breathing

it seems
and knowing

just how
much to give

in either
direction

without
breaking—

an exemplary
figure

perfectly
designed

to catch
and hold

small
insects

this
sunlight

my fluttering
attention.

Just This

Splash of
blood

red
quince

behind
the ash tree.

Bigleaf Maples

I like the way the roots of these bigleaf maple trees
muscle up through the ground like mountain ranges,
some of them with fern-moss forests on their slopes.
I step over them like a god bestriding the earth.

But when I crane my neck to look up, I see I cannot see
their crowns, so high are they, and to them I must seem
a needlessly complicated creature, one who walks
and thinks and worries and sometimes stops to look.

And now the roots look like cresting waves or ripples
over creek rocks, and the path becomes a stream.
I'm walking upstream, seen by the unseen.

Fall's Mirror

Flat on
my back

staring
up at

a map of
my own

mind the
elm tree's

black
branches—

nothing
left to

catch
the wind.

No-Self

I tell myself
there is

no self—
I am just

a place
where the

universe
happens

to be
happening

telling itself
through me.

Something and Nothing

There's something to be said
for having nothing to say,

though I don't know what
that is, or isn't, just as

there's something to be
known about not-knowing,

which I would tell you
if I could. There must be

something to be gained
by losing, a seed of victory

buried in every failure,
else I would not be here.

Clearly, there's something
to be desired about being

beyond desire, as the sages
never tire of telling us,

and nothing more fulfilling
than emptying yourself out—

no ground beneath your feet,
nothing to hold onto, no handrail,

no belief, only this bright,
self-sustaining air, and a falling

that feels like floating.

Passing Through

Nothing
sticks

to
space

everything
passes

right
through

leaving
and

leaving
no trace—

falling
stars and

flocks of
geese

a single
leaf

trains
of thought

and
real trains

threading
the

distance
their

mournful
honking in-

separable
from silence.

Above the Clackamas

I dip my mind
into the river

send my thoughts
downstream

in dissipating
swirls over

the temporary
eternity of rocks

I thought I
needed them

and sit between
two small fires

of Scotch Broom
bushes on

the bank
each petal tipped

with slanted
light

and there is
stillness here—

flowing going
nowhere clean.

Timely Question

How can time
be

rushing
by

and

standing
still

at the
same time?

On Turning Sixty-Four

The slowing down
is speeding up.

Four a.m.

Cat sniffs
the

candle
flame

then rubs
her

face
against

Tilopa's
Ganges

Maha-
mudra

while
outside

falling
through in-

finite space
is rain.

Morning, East Wallingford

Morning in East Wallingford,
not to be confused with
Wallingford proper,
down the road
a few miles
here in Vermont:
a bifurcated village.
Nothing much is
happening.
We had a thunderstorm
last night and now
bullfrogs are squawking
from the pond, as if
the storm had lodged
fragments of thunder
in their throats,
a wet and rubbery sound,
mildly insistent,
counterpointed by
faint birdsong
against a backdrop
of highway traffic,
cars and trucks,
the human contribution
to the soundscape.

The luna moth
we found last night
affixed to the porch railing
is gone, swept away by
the wind probably.
A fabulous creature,
green and leaflike,
with delicate orange ferns
for antennae and a curlicue
on each wing, added
for what purpose?
A mystery.
My wife is asleep upstairs,
her mother and father
a little further down the road.
I sit here feeling content,
even as I know the world
as we know it is ending,
happiness resting
in the pit of my stomach,
a calm excitement,
my mind free of anger,
resentment, ambition, regret.
Twelve raindrops hang
from the window sash,

gathering weight.
One or two look ready
to fall, but who
knows when
that will happen.
Pearled, light-filled,
each one a condensation
of cloud called downward
by invisible forces,
just as we are,
falling but not yet fallen,
held between earth
and sky, then and now,
and now the rain begins again.

Acknowledgments

My thanks to the editors of the following journals for first publishing some of the poems collected here.

Cloudbank: "Sleep Thief," "Fall's Mirror"

The Gettysburg Review: "Non-Harming," "Wishful Thinking"

Lion's Roar: "sleepless night"

The Manhattan Review: "The Things We Tell Each Other," "*Bomb Pops!*," "Design," "Steady Going," "Dharma Talk"

NOON: journal of the short poem: "Decomposition," "I put my glasses on," "feet hurt, back hurts," "Epistemologies"

Poetry Northwest: "Something and Nothing"

Rattle: "Morning, East Wallingford," "I put my glasses on," "the pain is still there," "coming unstitched," "fifty years ago," "not so different," "cold spring morning," "scattered crocuses"

Southern Poetry Review: "Flight Path"

The Sun Magazine: "Wanting Not Wanting," "On Turning Sixty-Four," "Timely Question," "Dudley Ball"

The Westchester Review: "Big Leaf Maples," "Emptiness Is Not Enough"

"Something and Nothing" and "Dharma Talk" appeared
in an earlier collection, *No Day at the Beach* (University of Wisconsin Press, 2020).

"Something and Nothing" was featured on *Verse Daily*,
https://www.versedaily.org/.

"Emptiness Is Not Enough" is for Ron Moshontz.
"Morning, East Wallingford" is for Chuck and Lore
Ferguson.
"Dharma Talk" is for Peter Williams.
"The Things We Tell Each Other" is for John Thomas.

I am extremely grateful to Heather Sellers, Andrea
Hollander, Paulann Peterson, and Alice Boyd for
offering helpful feedback on the entire manuscript.
I'd like to thank Justin Rigamonti and Fred Muratori
as well for astute responses to specific poems. Laura
Cunningham provided exactly the kind of sensitive
and supportive editing every poet hopes to receive. For
continuing to support my work and for bringing it so
beautifully into the world, I bow once again to Daniel
Aitken and the whole team at Wisdom Publications.

About the Author

 John Brehm is the author of three previous books of poetry: *Sea of Faith, Help Is on the Way*, and *No Day at the Beach*. He's also the author of a book of essays, *The Dharma of Poetry: How Poems Can Deepen Your Spiritual Practice and Open You to Joy*, and the editor of the bestselling anthology, *The Poetry of Impermanence, Mindfulness, and Joy*, both from Wisdom Publications. With his wife, Feldenkrais teacher Alice Boyd, he leads mindfulness retreats that incorporate Feldenkrais Awareness through Movement lessons, meditation, and mindful poetry discussions. He lives in Portland, Oregon, and can be found online at johnbrehmpoet.com.

What to Read Next from Wisdom Publications

The Dharma of Poetry
How Poems Can Deepen Your Spiritual Practice and Open You to Joy
John Brehm

"A warm invitation to explore the beauty of our own lives."—Joseph Goldstein

The Poetry of Impermanence, Mindfulness, and Joy
John Brehm

"This collection would make a lovely gift for a poetry-loving or dharma-practicing friend; it could also serve as a wonderful gateway to either topic for the uninitiated."—*Tricycle: The Buddhist Review*

Zen Master Poems
Dick Allen

"*Zen Master Poems* features reflection, meditation, mystery, humor, admonition, koans, calm observation, and Buddhist thought for readers and seekers on every path."—*Lion's Roar*

The Wisdom Anthology of North American Buddhist Poetry
Andrew Schelling

"Nothing else comes close."—*Pacific Rim Review of Books*

Awesome Nightfall
The Life, Times, and Poetry of Saigyō
William LaFleur

"The illuminated world that was called out by one man's lifetime of walking and meditation is again right here."—Gary Snyder

Everything Yearned For
Manhae's Poems of Love and Longing
Francisca Cho

Winner of the Daesan Foundation Literary Award

About Wisdom Publications

Wisdom Publications is the leading publisher of classic and contemporary Buddhist books and practical works on mindfulness. To learn more about us or to explore our other books, please visit our website at wisdomexperience.org or contact us at the address below.

Wisdom Publications
132 Perry Street
New York, NY 10014 USA

We are a 501(c)(3) organization, and donations in support of our mission are tax deductible.

Wisdom Publications is affiliated with the Foundation for the Preservation of the Mahayana Tradition (FPMT).